APQC'S PASSPORT TO SUCCESS SERIES

Corporate Training

A GUIDE FOR YOUR JOURNEY
TO BEST-PRACTICE PROCESSES

Marisa Brown

Paige Leavitt

Darcy Lemons

Wes Vestal

PUBLICATIONS

American Productivity & Quality Center
123 North Post Oak Lane, Third Floor
Houston, Texas 77024

Edited by Emma Skogstad
Designed by Connie Choate

Manufactured in the United States of America

ISBN 1-932546-38-3

American Productivity & Quality Center
Web site address: www.apqc.org

Contents

Acknowledgments

APQC would like to thank all of the organizations we have worked with to uncover the trends and best practices in the realm of corporate training. Without the companies that sponsor our research—and especially those that are willing to impart their knowledge, experiences, and insights—we would not be able to share this valuable knowledge with the public.

We extend a special thank-you to those organizations that sponsored the following benchmarking reports:

1. *Aligning Employee Learning with Corporate Strategy* (1999)
2. *Assessing Learning Outcomes* (1998)
3. *Developing Leaders at All Levels* (1999)
4. *Leadership Development: Building Executive Talent* (1999)
5. *Planning, Implementing, and Evaluating E-Learning Initiatives* (2002)
6. *Succession Management: Identifying and Cultivating Tomorrow's Leaders* (2001)
7. *Technology-based Training: Global Strategies for Learning* (1999)
8. *Technology-mediated Learning: Enhancing the Management Education Experience* (2000)
9. *The Corporate University: Learning Tools for Success* (1998)
10. *The Corporate University: Measuring the Impact of Learning* (2000)
11. *Today's Teaching and Learning: Leveraging Technology* (1999)

APQC would also like to thank those that participated as best-practice organizations and allowed our study participants to examine and learn from their corporate training practices. A significant amount of information in this book was gained during those benchmarking studies.

Preface:
Why Training Is Important

[handwritten: WHY DON'T THEY ALREADY KNOW?]

[handwritten: IS HUMANITY CAPITAL?]

Organizations are realizing that their most important assets are not equipment, technology, or machines but rather human capital and the know-how that resides in the minds of their employees. Employees' skill, innovation, and expertise form the *[handwritten: RELATIONAL SENSE?]* cornerstone of an organization's profitability and economic growth, hence the demand for a highly educated work force and for continual development of employee skills. Corporate training is an excellent way to maximize these valuable resources.

Corporate training efforts originate from a variety of needs, such as a need to serve internal customers, a rapidly changing customer and/or competitive environment, a need for cost savings, in anticipation of changing needs of an organization, and a push from senior management. Corporate training also allows organizations to unite dispersed work forces through standardized (and ideally, best) practices and present a knowledgeable, unified face to customers. Empowering employees to be more educated and responsive to customer needs, consequently, increases an organization's business opportunities.

In addition to its ability to affect business opportunities, corporate training also helps organizations address retention issues. In many cases, corporate training adds to the benefit package an organization offers its employees. It is also a critical aspect of new-hire development, succession management plans, and support to meet performance goals. With these drivers, organizations must train high-potential employees faster. Retirement is a huge, looming issue for many industries, and the need to train new employees or current

[handwritten: How? Some skills are acquired slower...]

employees in new jobs faster and better increases proportionately to the number retiring.

You will hear the statement again and again: In the future, learning will be the only source of competitive advantage. When it comes to developing employees, smart chief executives are making strategic investments to ensure their executives can produce strong results. Budget is not the only commitment.

WHAT DOE[S] THIS MEA[N] ?

By developing the ability of their work force to make quick, creative decisions that align with the companies' strategic values, organizations can strengthen their market positions, tackle current problems, and prepare for future challenges. Ultimately, corporate training is most direct way for an organization to ensure its work force is capable of meeting overarching strategic goals. Not having prepared the employees already in place can curb the potential growth of a business.

However, developing corporate training efforts through training activities and other learning opportunities cannot be simply a "cut-and-paste job." What may be considered a best practice for one company may be a not-so-good idea for another. Yet APQC has gleaned common insights from its benchmarking efforts that can serve as a starting point to effectively prepare the work force at all levels of an organization. This guidebook details:

- corporate training trends,
- creating a strategy,
- working with senior-level executives,
- designing and delivering learning opportunities,
- building relationships across the organization,
- marketing and communicating learning opportunities,
- creating a supportive learning environment,
- outlining expectations of employees/students,
- using evaluation data to remain relevant, and
- evolving and expanding corporate training efforts.

With relevant findings of organizations from 11 APQC benchmarking studies and useful examples from 20 best-practice organizations, this book can be used as a guide to best-practice processes for corporate trainers.

Corporate Training Trends

A number of exciting transformations in workplace management values and technology have created a need to revisit how organizations train employees. Traditional training has morphed into employee-driven and performance-focused experiences, often through a corporate university, performance consulting, or increasingly, through computer-based instruction.

There is greater discussion today about alternatives to traditional training than ever before. Interestingly though, executive leadership and the line workers are initiating this discussion, not the training function. Leadership in the public and private sector has stepped forward in recent years and proclaimed the need to get the most value out of an existing work force. The budgets allocated to training, development, and learning solutions continue to grow. In the United States, the direct expenditures for training and development exceed $100 billion in medium to large organizations, including the government sector. Data shows that budgets have increased each year, and similar trends have evolved in other countries. Meanwhile, training and organizational development functions are trying to control the runaway costs of facilities-based training or the transportation and opportunity costs of bringing employees to central training locations.

The ever-growing demand for current information and skills is an opportunity for employees to better serve their organizations through more flexible training strategies. Best-practice organizations are often shifting training from the category of an employee benefit cost that should be controlled to a business investment that should be focused and managed. As an investment, these initiatives require the participation of executive management and typically span many functions across the enterprise.

The employee, too, has more to say about how and when information and skill requirements need to be met, now that the Internet allows for convenience and choice. Training options now span time zones, and often languages, with 24-hour access and flexible communications strategies key to proper delivery. In most cases, employees "pull" the products they need instead of having central authorities push them.

Also affecting these other trends, technology-based training is the most important and most quickly evolving trend. Including computer-based training, performance support, satellite broadcast, and Web-based formats, these technologies complement or support learning that requires a facility.

As with all of the other ways technology has become part of our lives, the only thing that is sure to happen is change. Getting ahead of that change to make the most of it is a goal we all share.

Employee-driven Training

The focus of training and organizational development functions is shifting to performance improvement. The implementation of training solutions to improve job performance represents a tremendous change in the way these functions are organized, managed, and operated. Training and development's roles, skills, and outputs drastically change as staff members transform from their current roles into a group of capable performance improvement specialists and consultants. Trainers now facilitate learning processes to support employees' achievement, performance, and satisfaction. Because of this shift, employees now have a more active role in determining the selection and design of opportunities to learn.

From retraining internal staff to providing a help desk, best-practice organizations readily respond to employee needs, as demonstrated by best-practice organization IBM in the 2002 APQC benchmarking report *Planning, Implementing, and Evaluating E-Learning Initiatives*. IBM responds to changes in its employees' professional development needs in a variety of ways. In the early to mid-1990s, IBM faced financial difficulties, so it cut back on its education infrastructure and learning capabilities and froze hiring. In the later 1990s, IBM rebuilt its learning infrastructure and hired 50,000 additional employees. At this time, IBM recognized that its business was changing from a hardware producer to the services sector. As a result, IBM identified the need for employees to update skills quickly and also recognized that learning enhances business acumen. *WHAT SKILLS?*

IBM gained support for electronic learning by exhibiting lower costs, offering modularization (which permits targeted learning), and disrupting its employees' personal lives to a lesser degree. In most cases, IBM eliminates the classroom version of a course when its e-learning equivalent is created. IBM provides several standard e-learning products, services, and tools but does not require their use by employees.

The organization offers many types of learning opportunities to a diverse population, APQC reported in 2002. Fifty-five percent of employees have been at IBM less than five years, so it is a relatively young work force. Ninety-five percent of all employees have a computer. Forty-five percent are mobile employees. Most connectivity is through dial-in access, which can cause problems for employees dialing in from outside the United States. IBM provides employees with the option to download learning materials to their own desktop to operate in local mode. More than half of IBM's employees are not native speakers of English, so IBM must use audio and video selectively.

IBM uses a governance process that identifies and prioritizes development needs. A global learning council oversees the e-learning initiative. This governance process provides a funding model that is owned and operated by representatives of each IBM business unit.

In addition, each of IBM's five major business units and geographies has its own learning integrator, or executive. Individuals in the role of learning integrator prioritize learning investments that are common across business units. These individuals then represent the learning interests of their business unit or geography. Representatives from the different geographies address varying infrastructure needs and establish buy-in from each area. For example, they decide how much of an education budget is needed for the next year and where to spend it. They manage skills development and execution of the program within IBM infrastructure; they also develop the learning strategy. Learning integrators are the operational group for funding and were established by the global learning council. IBM's learning integrators help the organization keep its focus on the employees' needs.

A Shift Toward Both Performance Consulting and Corporate Universities

Organizations around the globe continue to adopt the corporate university concept. This concept involves a process—not necessarily a place—by which all levels of employees (and sometimes customers and suppliers) participate in learning experiences necessary to improve job performance and enhance business impact. Although the actual number of corporate universities is difficult to pinpoint, some estimate that more than 2,000 exist in the United States. More importantly, the trend continues to grow. It began in North America and has spread to Europe, Asia, and the rest of the world in a limited manner. Organizations have invested heavily in this concept, sometimes with a price as high as 5 percent of payroll compensation.

In this scenario, when an organizational needs assessment in performed, only those needs requiring a learning solution are funneled to corporate universities. Although this method has value, it cannot resolve problems that involve nontraining solutions. As a result, skill gaps within the organization continue to exist.

EXECUTIVES Corporate universities have recognized the need for a service to identify skill gaps and find solutions to fill these gaps outside of the traditional training model. The solution has been the establishment of performance consulting services in corporate universities or human resources departments. Performance consultants address performance issues that cannot be solved through traditional training methods. By working to resolve a problem without training, consultants bridge the gap between knowledge and application to improve performance.

Performance consulting services can significantly alter the structure and function of a corporate university. Figure 1, page 6, compares major differences between traditional corporate universities and those that offer performance consultants.

Best-practice organization National Security Agency provides performance consultations for its employees. The concept of performance consulting was first introduced at National Security Agency to effectively transfer training. As the managers at National Security Agency learned that seat-time in a training course did not always solve performance problems, they requested additional support. Performance consulting surfaced as an option that would save National Security Agency money by improving the work force or by at least avoiding excessive training costs.

The use of internal performance consultants was an added benefit because managers already understood National Security Agency's culture and values. These consultants—who have varied backgrounds and areas of expertise—can deliver multiple interventions to sustain large-scale cultural changes. Examples of these interventions include career development systems, communication systems, feedback systems, organizational design and

FIGURE 1: Difference Between Corporate University and Performance Consulting

Traditional corporate university characterized by:	Corporate university with a focus on performance improvement characterized by:
• No specific client relationship is established	• A client is served throughout the process
• No business need for programs	• Programs linked to specific business needs
• No assessment of performance deficiencies	• Assessment of performance and causes
• Most problems have training solutions	
• Services organized around design and delivery performance	• Full range of services of improve
• Specific objectives focus on learning	• Program objectives focused on job performance and business impact
• No effort to prepare the work environment to support transfer of learning performance	• Environment prepared to support transfer
• Typical job title includes the word *designer* or *trainer*	• Typical job title includes the words *performance consultant* or *performance technologist*
• Work activities focus on preparation and teaching	• Work activities focus on collaboration and consulting
• Communication outside the corporate university is limited	• Contacts outside the department are frequent and necessary
• No efforts to build partnership with key managers	• Partnerships established with key managers and clients
• Corporate university structure contains narrowly focused functions, such as development, delivery, and administration	• Corporate university structure contains broad-based functions, such as analysis, consulting, design, and facilitation
• Corporate university has a learning label and usually reports to a human resource executive	• Corporate university has a performance improvement label and usually reports to an operations executive
• No measurement of results or cost benefits analysis	• Measurement of results and cost benefit analyses are conducted regularly

development, and balanced scorecard consultation, as well as training solutions such as instructor-led training, technology-based training, and on-the-job training programs.

Technology-based Training

As the example from the National Security Agency illustrates, organizations have embraced ways for technology to support training. Originally, distance learning involved receiving a book in the mail. Later, there were correspondence courses. When computers became available, educators used this new means to deliver education at a distance. The next step in distance or simulated learning was technology-based training. Since its invention, the flight simulator has exemplified how technology can be used to provide relevant and cost-effective training. In the 1990s, many companies seized on this example and attempted to migrate and expand the concept into the private sector. The first organizations to plunge into these uncharted waters were members of an elite club: huge corporations with significant training budgets. Left out of the mix were a majority of other organizations that, for reasons of cost or complexity, chose instead to dabble in distance learning but with little strategy or purpose.

Today, using the Internet, corporate intranets, CD-ROMs, and videoconferencing, employees around the world are able to learn at a fraction of the time and cost. At first, the value of the computer may seem to be its ability to deliver information anytime and anywhere, but its value in education is potentially much more important. When the air flight simulator was invented, its important lay not its ability to be used in any remote location, but rather in its ability to enable one to learn to fly without risk, to accumulate the experience but never to be harmed by the experience. It was the beginning of simulated experiential learning.

In schools, experiential learning, or learning by doing, is rare because it is difficult to implement. The paradigm of a classroom of thirty students and one teacher does not lend itself to much interaction. No educator really believes that lecturing is the best means of education, but it is simply what is available in the classroom model. Attempts to simulate the classroom on a computer, therefore, are misguided.

E-learning can change the paradigm of learning and transform the lecture model into an interactive model. The computer can supplement the classroom with simulated experiences that allow students to learn by doing.

Businesses have begun to create high-quality training and deliver it in this new medium. Putting all of a company's training on a computer seemed possible only if the training was limited to questions and answers—to text followed by quizzes. But, as anyone who has crammed all night for an exam and promptly forgotten the material the next day realizes, passing tests and real education are not the same thing.

Employers want employees to learn to sell by selling, to learn to manage by managing, and to learn to help customers by helping customers. Once upon a time that is exactly how new employees learned their jobs. They were hired and they learned on the job. When training departments appeared on the scene, attempts were made to make what one needed to know on a job available in manuals and on tests. The premise was that telling people the facts of a situation can be a substitute for actually experiencing that situation. Unfortunately, nothing could be further from the truth. Learning on the job became an anathema, and learning in classrooms became the norm. It is no wonder corporate America was frustrated.

With the appearance of the Internet, corporations began to believe in e-learning as a new model for training. The Internet is an instantaneous medium. It is meant for people who want to learn right now and cannot wait. Yet, education does not lend itself to instant gratification. When you need to learn how to deal with a problematic customer, getting a little practice with a similar case might be a good idea if you have the time. And, if you want to learn how to sell a product, you will likely have to dedicate many hours learning to do so. In that case, you can wait a day to take a selling course, and Web delivery of such a course hardly matters.

The real issue with learning on the Web is money. Online courses are cheaper to deliver. They are also cheaper to build, but only because people seem willing to settle for so much less. Training departments that are trying to improve training suddenly find themselves trying to deliver all their training online. The corollary of the expectation that all of a company's training will be online is that the grand experiment of creating high-quality experiential training has been tabled. Faster and cheaper rarely means better, either in this arena or any other.

When planning an e-learning initiative, one should focus on content rather than delivery to maximize the educational advantages of eliminating classrooms. E-learning will dominate the learning arena when the virtual courses are interactive, engaging, authoritative, and relevant. A good course must motivate, enable inquiry, encourage reasoning, cause emotional impact, and most important, provide opportunities to practice. All of this is possible in e-learning.

A Strategic Approach

There is a clear link between business needs and strategies and the structure of a corporate training program. Of course, any organizational program should support a company's overall strategic efforts. But corporate trainers must ensure not only that the training program helps the organization meet its goals, but also that each and every course offering or service supports the strategy. To guarantee that corporate training proceeds with a thoughtful, strategic approach, this landmark will examine how to establish a lasting, powerhouse strategy that gains support from executives.

Creating a Strategy

By creating a training strategy based on the corporate strategy, organizations can capitalize on the opportunities afforded them by varied training solutions to enhance employee skills and knowledge in key strategic areas.

Key principles in developing a corporate training strategy follow.

- Start by developing a core philosophy of learning. For instance, Saturn's educational focus is organized around many different areas of training, each with its own planning and delivery processes. The core philosophy of learning is "to provide opportunities for all team members to learn, grow, and continuously improve."

- Then, gauge the mission, values, and culture of the organization so that the corporate training strategy can accurately reflect it. Adhering to a model of what corporate trainers traditionally do is far less important than creating a training program that reflects and reinforces the culture, mission, and values of the company.
- Make your overarching goals explicit: corporate training is a primary way to achieve an organization's strategic vision. Clearly define how the training program will add value in terms of providing consistent capabilities, reinforcing company values, and accelerating business strategies by focusing on the key asset—people.

Strategic drivers may include an organization-wide need to standardize messages delivered to employees or simply have a more productive work force than competitors. It is important to determine training goals—and their related requirements—only after identifying the expected outcomes. Instead of creating a strategic goal of every employee earning so many continuing education credits, focus on why the credits are required. What are core competencies needed from the work force? What about management?

Set goals that ultimately aim to improve business but are specific to match key business concerns, such as the retention and recruiting of employees and the learning process itself. Many times the goals reflect lessons derived from past training programs and efforts. The ultimate goal is usually a well-rounded combination of traditional classroom teaching and cutting-edge learning technologies that maximize the benefits of each method.

Examples from APQC's benchmarking studies follow to illustrate how strategies are set.

Saturn Corp. has a strategy based on both organization and industry needs. Union leadership actually works in conjunction with

TRAVELER'S TIP

Potential areas to establish core competencies:

- Business and technical knowledge
- Coaching and development
- Communication
- Customer satisfaction
- Innovation
- Interpersonal effectiveness
- Leadership learning
- Market focus
- Teamwork and collaboration
- Value creation

Saturn management to make business decisions. And education plays a significant role in the culture and strategy of the organization. The business strategy for the entire organization is to build good cars, focus on the customer, and empower the employee. Training is designed to increase the depth and breadth of people's talent. Saturn's corporate training function encompasses four main areas that address different parts of the business and its different customers: retail training, supplier training, "car builder" training, and consulting services.

In another example, Booz Allen Hamilton's Center for Performance Excellence aligns all of its learning strategies directly to its five strategic business areas: financials, technology, new/emerging markets, organizational changes, and business strategies. Whenever it takes on a new initiative, such as e-learning, it must determine which business areas it should align with and how the alignment will be accomplished. This alignment is strategic for the center because each business area has a senior vice president, or partner, who is assigned as the champion of that area. By linking into one of these areas, the center realizes a twofold benefit. First, this guarantees it is doing the right thing for the firm. Second, it helps the center build strong champions across the firm for it to get the funding it needs for activities and initiatives.

Example Missions

The mission for Booz Allen Hamilton's e-learning initiative is "to enable students, regardless of their physical location in the firm, to actively participate in best-in-class learning that enables absolute best performance, as judged by the firm's clients. We do this by delivering learning as close to the point of performance as possible, expanding learning across time, and targeting those competencies or employee levels for which ROI will be the greatest."

Eddie Bauer defines its corporate university by its mission: "accelerating the success of the company's business strategies by integrating associate performance with team excellence." Eddie Bauer University (EBU) has foundation programs in place for associates in its corporate offices, retail stores, and catalog call center. Its core philosophy of learning builds off this definition and emphasizes that learning is driven by the associate.

Support from Senior-level Executives

From the example of Booz Allen Hamilton, it is clear that what drives the emphasis and continued support of learning and education is a cultural commitment to the development of people. This commitment is set at the senior level.

It has been said before: senior-level support is critical for new organizational initiatives, particularly ones that impact the culture of the organization and change the face of the workplace. Without this support from the top, initiatives such as these will collapse and disappear because there is no momentum to keep them going.

In some cases at best-practice organizations APQC has bench-marked, senior management actually drove the implementation of the corporate training effort, primarily by naming leadership or giving shape to the organization in its early stages. In others, management has given strong financial support even during economic downturns. The following list shows some of the key measurement and evaluation roles of executives and managers.

1. Develop or approve a mission for the corporate training effort.
2. Allocate the necessary funds for successful training programs.
3. Allow employees time to participate in training programs.
4. Become actively involved in training programs and require others to do the same.
5. Support the corporate training efforts and ask other managers to do so.
6. Position corporate training in a visible and high-level place on the organization chart.
7. Require that each training activity be evaluated in some way.
8. Insist that programs be cost effective and require supporting data.
9. Set an example for self-development.
10. Create an atmosphere of open communication with corporate university leadership.

The key to gaining senior-level support is establishing a training strategy that supports the strategy senior managers have set for the entire organization. It is also helpful to ensure that training is accountable to senior management through advisory boards, metrics, and reporting relationships. When the training program is willing to hold itself up to scrutiny through whatever means senior managements finds appropriate, APQC has found that senior management is typically more willing to demonstrate its support through sustained funding, testimonials, and use of related products and services, as the following example will demonstrate.

At Procter & Gamble, key sponsors of the e-learning initiative include the chief information officer, the vice president of global business solutions, senior HR executives, the board of learning, and other vice presidents and general managers in the organization. For instance, the chief information officer provided the funding for an initial implementation of e-learning tools, whereas the vice president of global business solutions provided IT support and the capital to purchase the learning management system and live-distance licenses. For its e-learning initiative, the senior HR executives allowed the e-learning team to pursue the vision, and other vice presidents and general managers supported development and deployment of the Web-based college. Finally, Procter & Gamble's learning and knowledge council provided the funding for implementing the corporate training portal; the council is a group of senior executives who provide funding for innovative projects pertaining to learning and knowledge management.

Additionally, Procter & Gamble's board of learning works collaboratively to identify and deliver the learning to meet the needs of the various businesses worldwide. The board is made up of deans, each of whom represents a different global business unit, market development organization, global business system, and corporate function in Procter & Gamble.

Directions for Your Journey

- Lay the groundwork for corporate training. Be sure the training strategy has strong ties to organizational strategies and competencies.

- Ensure senior leadership support. Whether the initiative is driven by senior leaders or not, visible support in the form of funding, resources, facilitation, and testimonials goes a long way toward demonstrating credibility.

- Perform an organizational readiness assessment for training. Ensure the success of the initiative by assessing cultural, infrastructure, and employee readiness for more aggressive learning opportunities.

Developing a Program

A successful corporate training program engages the work force by offering a relevant learning experience where action, not knowledge, is the ultimate goal. Developing such a program involves designing appropriate learning opportunities and then effectively delivering them. In respect to design, this landmark focuses on identifying the target audience for training, selecting an approach and training activities, using vendors, and breaking down the teaching process. In respect to delivery, this landmark focuses on the new demands of leveraging technology.

Designing Learning Opportunities

The first step in designing learning opportunities is identifying target audiences. Training is most effective when it is adapted to its audience. For instance, a corporate training program may offer different learning opportunities for those struggling to meet annual performance goals, high-potential candidates in an executive-bound succession management effort, managers moving into a new operational area, new hires that are unfamiliar with the corporate culture, and recent graduates.

To determine which audiences currently need assistance for the organization to meet its strategic goals, the corporate training function should institute regular meetings to review organizational needs, as well as to review how current target audiences are responding to the learning opportunities. By involving HR, the senior-level champion, and representatives from business units that receive training, corporate trainers can objectively outline who needs training and what the organization's priorities are in delivering that training.

Dell, for instance, has two talent pools that break down into corporate level pools (global corporate talent) and business unit level pools (functional high-potential employees). Employees designated as global corporate talent are profiled and consist of individuals (fewer than 100) who can run significant portions of a function or business and can leverage skills or experience on a global basis. The company uses a concept called scaling to identify an individual's ability to grow into a higher-level job or scale with the growth of the current job. Individuals are designated as one of five ratings for potential:

1. promotable,
2. develop in place,
3. contribute in place (struggling, but manager willing to invest more time),
4. manage out of position, and
5. too new to call.

A designation on this scale determines what corporate training opportunities are appropriate for individual employees.

Sonoco uses eight talent pools that are divided by division and position when determining appropriate learning opportunities:

1. country managers (foreign countries),
2. vice president/director level for sales and marketing,
3. manager level for sales and marketing,
4. vice president/director level for manufacturing,

5. finance/IT positions,
6. human resources,
7. technology and engineering, and
8. purchasing and other staff pools.

Once the target audience is identified, the corporate trainers can select and design appropriate learning opportunities. There is no universal process map for designing corporate training. The design process, whether it be for discrete courses or entire learning programs, is thought by many to be the scientific part of the learning process in the corporate university. Heavy competition plays out each year for the top designers from recognized universities in the field of instructional design, such as Florida State and Syracuse.

Despite this emphasis, best-practice organizations APQC has benchmarked appear to have no universal process map for designing learning interventions. From needs analysis to course design and development to the eventual delivery, each organization remains distinct. Although this may seem to make the entire design process more complicated, this trend actually points to a positive result: business needs drive the design process. No standard design process works in every organization, but these organizations must maintain the flexibility to adapt to the changing demands of their business environments.

Although most best-practice organizations APQC has benchmarked continue to use traditional classroom training, there is a growing use of special assignments, active learning, and Web-based courses. (Technology also offers considerable potential in maintaining the ability to monitor developmental activities, which is discussed later.) Many organizations have been drawn to non-classroom education solutions for a wide range of reasons. On one end of the spectrum, an organization may be trying to reduce the costs associated with the classroom model. On the other end, the move to other delivery channels fits hand-in-glove with a business

A Blended Approach

Although the Bank of Montreal has made great strides in the technology-based training arena, it has not forsaken the classroom as a tool for change. Envisioned as part of the chairman's call for ongoing renewal, its Institute for Learning provides an important symbol of the bank's commitment to classroom learning. It offers classrooms with the best of learning technology, a high-tech business information center, breakout rooms, and role-play rooms outfitted with audiovisual equipment. Wide-open spaces, natural light, and a wellness center help to inspire energy, enthusiasm, and imagination among employees. Although the organization will continue to do more training through technology, the institute's facility will always be central to the bank's attempts to develop a learning culture.

imperative to expand the head count and span the globe with short cycle time. Organizations in the former category talk about how they are going to break away from the brick-and-mortar facility and create virtual universities at a fraction of the cost. Organizations in the second category give their salespeople CD-ROMs to use in their spare time and send their central business-unit executives to a negotiations course with experts.

However, technology-based training is not the be-all, end-all for training needs. Different material and content is best taught in different ways, so corporate trainers should use blended approaches to deliver learning in the most effective way. Best-practice organizations value a mixture of face-to-face and technology-based training offerings. Some topics are best learned face-to-face, and secondary benefits arise from high-touch experiences including networking and acculturation. Likewise, many subjects are learned better outside of the classroom and closer to the context where they will be applied.

In addition to training, most of these organizations use a variety of developmental activities such as mentoring, coaching, job rotation, traditional educational programs, and formalized feedback processes to engage their work force in developmental activities. It is important to consider traditional corporate training in this context to efficiently meet the organization's needs.

Examples follow to illustrate the variety of design approaches available.

Dow Chemical has identified numerous universities across the country that specialize in areas such as entrepreneurialism, technology, and international affairs. Dow Learning Centers worldwide have classroom activities and some select university business programs at graduate level. The programs are typically one to four weeks at universities such as University of Michigan, Indiana University, IMD, INSEAD, and the Thunderbird Institute. Dow also takes advantage of consortium programs (several companies jointly cooperating in an academic program). Dow also extensively uses Web-based functions to support people leaders and development, as well as an externally developed online learning and training program offering more than 600 courses. Examples of training courses available on the site include safety training, an executive-required course on respect and responsibility training, and compensation planning tools.

PanCanadian offers an internal MBA program called the management forum. The purpose of this two-year program is to provide management education by bringing best practices to participants. The management forum was specifically created to align management competencies with strategic direction to meet current and future needs. PanCanadian uses the forum to share existing knowledge and new findings. The forum is focused on developing three core competencies: performance management, change and innovation, and knowledge management.

Abbott Laboratories works to improve the performance of all employees through training and provides courses specifically for senior management. Also, several departments at Abbott Laboratories dedicate an internal coach trained in soft skills (listening, negotiation, etc.) to assist with development. These coaches help put together development and action plans, act as resources for a group, serve as group facilitators, and help reinforce the department's leadership curriculum. As the programs move up the seniority level, Abbott includes more access to the senior leaders of the organization, action learning and real business issue problems, and coaching opportunities. Its "management challenge" typically takes place 10 to 12 years into the job and is designed for the top 2,000 people in the organization. Individuals must be nominated and chosen for this program by their operating division president and the leadership development program. This two-week program exposes leaders to a variety of skills, programs, and activities to bolster their knowledge and abilities. Its leadership development program is for those leaders who will become executives in the organization, typically the top 600 people in the organization. It is a three-week program taken over the course of a year that includes action learning, time with the officers of the company and a variety of program challenges and opportunities to help these candidates learn and practice real leadership. Both programs require significant outlays of money and executive time, so they are reserved for those employees considered as potential executives of the next generation.

Another consideration in selecting and developing learning opportunities is the concept of action learning, which is the use of real-time business issues as the basis for learning and development. With this approach, content is not sacrificed for simplistic solutions; the answers to tough questions are not in the instructor's head but rather must be developed on the spot by the employees in training. By charging these individuals with the job of implementing their recommendations to solve actual business problems, corporate trainers deliver a learning experience that is tailored to both the organization and the employee's own development. In the end, action learning can be complicated and costly but very effective. Examples of action learning follow.

Eli Lilly believes that 70 percent of learning takes place on the job and has a robust active learning program. Its executive active learning program is an annual program that centers around 18 potential executive leaders who come from all functions. The structured program covers a six-week time frame, and the CEO chooses the business issue. Activities include off-site meetings and presentations by subject matter experts and team-based interviews with best-practice organizations, customers, and thought leaders. The results of the interviews are then compiled, and a presentation of findings to the CEO is generated, complete with a recommended course of action.

Although action learning is not frequently used at FedEx, the company does lean heavily on its executives to teach various courses and set the standard for leadership development. Its leadership institute teaches important management and leadership principles to new managers, senior managers, and directors. Employees benefit from classes taught by the CEO, the chief operating officer, and the chairman.

You will note in many of these examples that big ticket learning opportunities—such as external coaching, action learning, and external executive programs—are reserved for more senior leaders and those deemed high potential. Development tools that require intensive resources (both dollars and/or time of senior management) are reserved for candidates at more senior levels.

The most successful of these courses, APQC has found, are actually taught by executives. Using current leaders to teach potential leaders is crucial and has a number of advantages. First, it fosters open, two-way communication. Most leaders find that the time they spend teaching is time well spent. It helps them learn about the day-to-day activities and major concerns of the organization. In turn, the students gain organizational knowledge outside the formal channels.

Second, using current leaders establishes credibility. These leaders bring a believable, real-world approach to their students and serve as role models, helping to model the behavior being developed. Third, using leaders to teach leadership relays the expression of support by higher levels in the organization. This sends a strong message and underscores its importance. Finally, leaders teaching leadership helps to develop internal networks. Current leaders receive an opportunity to learn who the up-and-coming leaders are. The students make important and necessary contacts and learn whom to call on for help in the future.

The executive development programs at Abbott Laboratories depend heavily on the involvement of current leaders. The faculty mixture of academicians, industry experts, outside executives, and Abbott executives helps to broaden the offerings and appeal of the courses. Specifically, the inclusion of the CEO, the chief operating officer, and the chief financial officer in the courses, both in teaching and in more informal informational sessions, helps the programs focus on the business issues that are most important to Abbott Laboratories. These leaders teach a case study based on a current activity taking place in their divisions that gives the up-and-coming leaders an opportunity to affect the business and learn new skills and competencies in the process. HR also schedules dinners, outings, and group meetings with the CEO and executives to encourage these leaders to cultivate the relationships that help them run the businesses more smoothly and efficiently.

An additional consideration in designing courses (and later in delivering those courses) is to take advantage of third-party course providers with solutions that can be deployed throughout the organization. Evaluating whether to "build or buy" a training product is a common issue most organizations ponder when determining how to meet their training needs. Gaps in learning opportunities can be supplemented by licensing extensive libraries of courses from several vendors and distributing them at negligible cost via intranets or the Internet. But off-the-shelf courses can be too generic to be effective; as a result, flexibility and a willingness to listen are key traits to look for in a supplier.

It is easiest to buy courses from a vendor. However, these courses will be generic in nature. Generic courses are fine when you are talking about subjects that are invariant across organizations, but there are fewer of these than you might think. Math is math anywhere, of course, but marketing and sales can differ from place to place. Using the experience and methodologies particular to your organization may make it worthwhile to consider another choice.

Selecting courses that are built specifically for your company by a company devoted to the subject may be a better choice. It is also the most expensive choice. Is it worth it? It is when the knowledge being communicated to your employees is seen as critical to the organization's strategy.

The third choice is typically the best choice but the most difficult to implement. Creating an in-house group who can create high-quality training will greatly benefit the company who can afford this approach. An organization with a long-term focus on a specific activity needs to foster a group of people who can keep inventing new training.

For example, due to cost, the Army National Guard typically uses in-house resources if they exist and then turns to vendors or contractors for the expertise that may be lacking or unavailable. For commercial courseware, the Army National Guard negotiates with commercial vendors to secure technology-based courses that can be delivered over the Guard's distance learning network on a fee-for-use basis. Here, the first priority is to buy a commercial off-the-shelf product if one exists. The Guard negotiates a contract with a computer-based training vendor to offer an extensive library of IT training courses. If the Guard decides to go the route of a commercial vendor to develop a custom application, then an appropriate mix of educationally sound, quality products and cost is considered before any contract award. Authorware standards are also important; the Guard may often mix and match separate modules from different

TRAVELER'S

TIP

Philosophy on Vendors

QUALCOMM tries to buy most of its training programs off the shelf. If the proper material is not available from a vendor, then its learning center has to decide whether materials should be internally developed right away or if it can wait until there is an overwhelming need to develop them. In most cases, in-house development is done because the culture of the organization is to be ahead of the curve—to have the latest, greatest, and fastest item on the engineer's desktop. The general belief at QUALCOMM is that if the company is going to produce leading-edge technology, then its employees must do it with the best tools.

courses, so it is essential that all technology-based training adhere to certain standards. Generally, the National Guard works hard to hold contractors accountable for performance. Over time, the Guard has found that if a contractor is not on schedule after 15 percent of the project has been completed, then that contractor will probably be over budget and over schedule for the rest of the program. As a result, the National Guard now dismisses anyone who fails to stay on task early in the process.

Honeywell has adopted the policy of buying off the shelf whenever possible. There is little that Honeywell can add to a "visual basic" course, for example, to justify the huge additional cost of self-development. Where there are proprietary software issues and vendors cannot be used, the organization tries to rely on screen-cams with narration and lectures provided by senior Honeywell engineers. Honeywell's technology education center has two libraries of Internet-based training, one for end-user software training and the other for computer programmers. Because the center operates on a zero-budgeting model, it has to be careful when structuring arrangements with new vendors. If a course is not popular, then it will make the corporate trainers' task of recovering all costs that much harder. As a result, the manager of the center tries to negotiate per-person usage agreements with vendors. To have the vendors agree to such a contract, Honeywell's technology education must show what kind of internal marketing tools it has at its disposal.

Johnson & Johnson prefers to partner with a few suppliers it respects and knows. The company looks for suppliers that mesh well with its culture and seeks to develop long-term relationships with them. Johnson & Johnson also looks for suppliers that have content knowledge and are willing to go the extra mile to meet the company's specific needs. Suppliers are used for everything ranging from the design and development of corporate training programs to the actual delivery of these programs.

The discussion of designing traditional and untraditional courses, with and without vendors, points toward a pervasive trend in corporate training: the responsibility of selecting and design-ing learning opportunities is typically spread out over a number a people. With HR, senior management, and the corporate trainers keeping an eye on meeting the organization's strategic needs in a spectrum of opportunities, a course instructor now rarely decides all issues related to content selection, instructional design, delivery, and assessment. For example, faculty may identify the content, the learning objectives, and competencies that students need to develop, but an instructional designer may be the one who actually designs the instructional events and their sequencing, the packaging of the content, and the exercises. Yet another person may be the multimedia developer who translates the course into an online environment, and a fourth person may actually deliver the course.

At Ernst & Young, LLP Global Learning Solutions, for example, several individuals and departments perform the teaching process. Many courses were developed internally, using Ernst & Young subject matter experts. At Global Learning Solutions, instructional designers, graphic artists, and project managers participate in the design of various courses. Some subject matter experts write instructional material, and instructional designers check to make sure the information is appropriate. However, instructional designers usually write the material. Responsibility for course content has been pushed out to the business units within Ernst & Young, with Global Learning Solutions representatives working with the various units to help them keep the course modules up-to-date. Internal Ernst & Young subject matter experts are responsible for reviewing the course content that the business units and Global Learning Solutions create. At Ernst & Young, independent contractors called knowledge workers produce online course.

Directions for Your Journey

- Carefully assess both the need for technology and the technology available before adding new capabilities to the portfolio.
- Develop a single, integrated learning portal for professional development.
- Demonstrate a combination of delivery approaches for e-learning solutions.

Delivering Learning Opportunities

One of the most important aspects of training design is a solid understanding of the training delivery environment. This is true of the traditional classroom and printed training, as well as the many alternatives technology brings. Proper design consideration has at least two dimensions:

1. developing an understanding of audience needs and constraints that will affect the uptake of the training and
2. designing a solution to exploit the strength of the delivery channel.

With the principles of classroom delivery well-established among corporate trainers, this section will focus on newer demands in delivering learning opportunities with the assistance of technology.

Most organizations move their existing training online because it saves money and allows training to occur anytime and anywhere. There is nothing wrong with the desire to save money, but putting training in a book would save money as well. The reason training has been held in classrooms is that people believed that classroom training worked better than simply asking employees to read a training manual. The purpose of classrooms has been to provide a better learning experience than a manual could provide. Different media require different methods.

TRAVELER'S TIP

There are a plethora of options for technology-based training delivery, from videotape to virtual meeting places made possible by Web technologies. It is useful to sort the options for technology-based training along the dimensions of delivery, time, and place interactions.

Traditional classroom models are same-time/same-place solutions, whereas broadcasts of lectures to multiple sites are same-time/different-place solutions. Both are considered synchronous because the student and instructor experiences are tightly coupled. Many technologies support this delivery style, including satellite/videoconference classrooms and real-time Web classroom discussion/presentation environments. The instructional designs in these synchronous venues often include lectures/presentations or live discussion about a topic.

The alternative asynchronous model includes experiences that can take place at different times/in the same place, such as taking a computer-based training course at home over several sessions, or at different times/in different places, such as taking a computer-based training course on a plane and in a hotel. The instructional design ranges from purely self-study experiences through extended multiple-person-interaction-over-time solutions. The asynchronous solutions have been demonstrated by best-practice organizations benchmarked by APQC to be the most successful approaches.

When books were introduced to classrooms, they were initially simply read to the assembled students, hence the word *lecture*. Then, new teaching methodologies evolved that were more appropriate to classrooms, and books became supplemental materials for teachers.

The key question to ask is why the Internet might be a better medium for training and what kind of training would work best online. Although saving money is important, the real savings will take place only if employees learn faster or better. Giving them the same text on screen that they could have had in a book may not accomplish this purpose. Making training into an endless quiz may not accomplish this purpose. Training should look as much as possible like the real job experience an employee might encounter.

Pervasive computing and communication technologies are a prerequisite to developing and sustaining online learning opportunities. Pervasive computing and communication environments are defined in this context as individual, convenient access to a networked computer (typically a laptop computer). Most initiatives in the best-practice organizations APQC has benchmarked require students to access a laptop computer. Instructors and, in some cases, staff members may also need continuous and convenient access to a networked computer.

In addition to computer usage, the standardization of hardware and software applications is a critical prerequisite. Corporate trainers may not be sure whether hardware and software applications are standardized, or possibly what is even available. Therefore, it is important to begin the effort to deliver technology-mediated learning opportunities by assessing the technology available and the additional technology needed to deliver specific courses and activities.

Working collaboratively with the IT function, corporate trainers should fully assess both the need for technology and the technology available before adding new items to the technology portfolio. By assessing the current technology, an organization should identify what type of technology would work best in light of company culture and user capability. Figure 2 presents common criteria

Common Criteria

1. Product support (e.g., help desk)
2. Speed (ability for student to get skilled quickly)
3. Financial stability of vendor
4. Credibility of expert content source
5. Level of interactivity
6. User-friendly
7. Ability to customize
8. Price

Figure 2

used when selecting appropriate vendors, with the most important being product price and whether it is user-friendly. Other criteria include the ability of the application to work in the organization's existing infrastructure, compliance with standards, and fit with the organization's learning strategies and guidelines.

The following examples provide details on how best-practice organizations benchmarked by APQC assess the available technologies in relation to the cultural and technological needs of their technology-mediated learning opportunities.

At General Motors University (GMU), the key to designing an e-learning initiative is assessing and selecting the delivery platform. Presently, the Internet is the primary medium for new courses, and asynchronous delivery is the chief mode of learning.

While designing and developing e-learning, GMU recognized that it is important to have Web standards. The GM team developed comprehensive Web standards documents to address topics, such as ISD principles, to incorporate into this type of training and screen interfaces. If purchasing software off the shelf or developing a course internally, then the team uses two course selection tools: its technology matrix (to assess infrastructure) and its content matrix (to assess quality). The technology matrix assesses items such as company strength, manageability, interoperability, usability, industry standards, and capability and was used by the team to determine what e-learning tools to use. The content matrix is a course quality and effectiveness evaluation tool, which categorizes instructional design, navigation, assessment, and support. Both matrices include questions such as:

- Are the objectives clearly written?
- Do the objectives meet the business needs they are looking for?
- Does the course engage the student in meaningful, skill-based activities?

According to GMU, e-learning brings certain additional challenges to the content design and development process. Traditional classroom learning outcomes need to be replicated in any e-learning activities offered. And e-learning does not provide the social interaction provided in a face-to-face environment.

In another example, with the help of consultants, Procter & Gamble identified the appropriate tools to make e-learning a reality. It selected SABA as the learning management system, Centra Symposium as a live-distance learning tool (virtual classroom), and Trivantis Lectora as the authoring tool for Web-based training. With these tools established, Procter & Gamble proceeded to focus on its design strategy, which was to direct traffic to the RapidLEARN Web site (its online learning portal).

A key component of Procter & Gamble's e-learning design process was to ensure that the applications performed well in the existing structures. The technology infrastructure for e-learning was developed by the IT application development groups who worked closely with the business units. Its global learning IT group performed a range of responsibilities that included:

- leading the efforts on vendor evaluations,
- conducting the standard certification processes to ensure Procter & Gamble's preferred products would run in the intranet and other standard workstation platforms,

TRAVELER'S TIP

QUALCOMM uses a number of tools to determine the best medium for delivering courses. One of these tools is the training medium checklist created by the Masie Center, a think tank located in Sarasota Springs, N.Y. The instrument goes through the requirements of the subject, the location of employees, the type of skills being taught, and the level of interaction required to determine whether a course should be lecture based or whether an online format is appropriate. If possible, QUALCOMM's learning center tries to make classroom training and technology-based training options available for all of its courses. Even when learning takes place in a traditional classroom, all of the training material is available online to class participants before a class begins. In addition, the group uses technology to distribute preliminary assignments—a set of tools students should review before they come to class so that everyone can start at the same level and time is not wasted reviewing old material.

- ensuring application security standards are met, and
- working with the central IT function to install the learning management system and distance-learning tool.

Procter & Gamble wanted to provide a variety of authoring tools that are easy for the nonprogrammer to use, yet flexible and powerful enough for the technically capable. It was also important that the tools adhered to industry standards while providing templates and design guidelines.

Although Procter & Gamble supports some consistent tools in authoring, live-distance, templates, and other e-learning support mechanisms, instructional methods vary by the course developer in a given business unit. Procter & Gamble has not driven a particular instructional methodology, so ownership of content and training remains in the business units. Off-the-shelf content was tested for user friendliness and content alignment, and business units conducted their own user testing and monitored feedback from users.

Potential Delivery Tools

- Web-enhanced face-to-face courses
- Satellite TV
- Student-owned laptops in class
- Classrooms with networked computers;
- Web-based discussion groups
- Videoconferencing
- Desktop videoconferencing
- Training CD-ROMs
- E-mail
- Networked computer labs
- Classroom computer projection systems
- Utilization of online commercial databases
- Groupware
- Listserv/Bulletin board/Electronic discussion environment
- Online library databases (beyond catalog)

In terms of vendor management, Procter & Gamble asked the vendors to describe the top courses they offered around Procter & Gamble's core competencies. They then asked global learning managers to use their expertise in a given area to determine which courses were best.

Whatever technology-mediated training activities are decided on, it is often helpful to deliver them through a single, integrated corporate training portal. This way, employees can turn to one consolidated source for all of their learning needs, from individual development plans to career road maps. Learning portals tend to have a consistent look and feel throughout their sections (in keeping with the organization's image) and often feature similar icons to ease the user's navigation around the site.

For example, IBM provides a global intranet site that compiles resources in one central location for employee skills development.

Called "CareerPlanner," it presents information and tools needed by employees to plan and grow in their current career and also for them to explore other available career opportunities. The portal is composed of a section on information and a section containing tools. The information side provides the employee development cycle, career descriptions, thousands of career road maps, information on distributed learning, internal organization pages, career talks, and a professional leadership technical exchange, which provides lectures. Since 1997 IBM has developed career road maps for all professions, from electrical engineers to sales representatives. Skill road maps chart the progression of a typical career path and provide critical links to learning solutions via an online learning portal.

On the tools side, IBM's intranet portal provides links to individual development plans, personal skills updates, and mentoring and will soon provide job postings. Employees can assess skills by responding to a series of questions, download an individual development plan form, choose a mentoring approach, and select skill development road maps. Most professions at IBM have a defined skill set, and CareerPlanner details the skill sets for 18 different career areas. The CareerPlanner site is increasingly tailored according to geographic differences in services and access. IBM built the tools found in CareerPlanner internally.

Career road maps, which provide employees with the learning activities to grow in a given profession or job, can also be found on the intranet site and are broken down by career, industry, skills, organizations, systems offerings, and solutions. Subject matter experts or career leaders regularly update content found on the road maps. The road maps suggest books, courses, and conferences to help employees succeed in their careers.

By providing the employee development cycle on the CareerPlanner intranet portal, IBM helps engage the employee and manager in effective career discussions. Steps in the cycle are to:
- establish personal business commitment objectives,
- assess skills and competencies (via direct link to skill assessment),

- update individual development plans,
- execute individual development plans (e.g., attend a course),
- have an individual development plan checkpoint, and
- determine overall personal business commitment ratings.

In addition to a portal, it is important to consider what other support tools will be both helpful and realistic. The research on learning complex concepts through interactive 3D visualization is compelling. However, when virtual reality technologies finally moved down from military prices toward the business capital budget range (a desktop 3D system was at the business platform price point in 1997), the training industry did not experience the revolution predicted. Why? Training that requires 3D accelerators and joysticks to operate is not useful to students who work with a simple keyboard and mouse at their desk. Another less exotic example: Videotape courses do not typically enjoy volumes of students comparable to classroom courses despite identical content. Again, most organizations do not deploy VCRs and monitors as part of other vital daily processes, so the technology becomes a barrier. Using the workplace platform as the filter, it quickly becomes evident that the most effective training technologies are those that employees and businesses use every day.

Even the basic technologies, however, often require special skills in the development environment (knowledge of digital video compression, programming skills, server administration, etc.). Keeping a group of diverse specialists actively employed throughout the year requires an organization to commit to a minimum critical mass of activities. It also establishes an upper limit on the amount of course development that can be achieved. It is important to have flexible head count models that include a core number of managers and designers and a network of supporting specialists on their teams. Additional resources for projects are hired from the outside or are "borrowed" from another internal function when the need arises.

For technology-mediated training activities, it is important to staff the training functions with instructional designers or faculty members who know how to get the most out of their media. Teaching in an online environment, for instance, requires different skills and approaches than teaching in a traditional classroom. For example, many instructors initially find it challenging to facilitate discussions in online classes. Verbal and nonverbal cues that are used to convey information and meaning in face-to-face environments cannot be used in online, text-only interactions. Many experts point out that classroom environments introduce a level of control and certainty that is at risk when considering solutions that do not include "captivity." Other interpretations for the success of classroom models include student incentive to get away from the job and the creation of a distraction-free environment. Regardless of the specific reasons, it is clear that distance solutions that do not include facilities and scheduling often require a different standard for experience quality or consequence.

In conclusion, in creating a culture pervaded by the use of technology, many of the best-practice partners benchmarked by APQC have developed a wide range of strategies for supporting technology-based training activities. These approaches include:

- a strong strategic plan in which the use of technology for teaching plays a prominent role;
- extensive investment in technology infrastructure;
- support from senior leadership for the use of technology in teaching;
- support for faculty members who seek to use technology in the form of project funding, release time, technical support, computer allocations/upgrades, and instruction; and
- support for students through computer access, Internet accounts, and financial support.

TRAVELER'S TIP

Saturn training is delivered by process owners and internal SMEs. Internally there are different deliverers: facilitators, coaches, instructors (i.e., focused on technical and quality concerns), teachers (human skills courses), and trainers in training. In addition, leaders at Saturn are not just asked to teach; they are required to do so. Teaching, or facilitating training, is counted as training hours for the leaders. Saturn uses this model to capitalize on the knowledge that exists in the company.

Whereas each of these approaches individually can create a positive atmosphere for faculty instructional development, the combination of them appears to result in a culture that is totally immersed in teaching and learning with technology. These best-practice organizations kept their focus on teaching and learning issues, rather than on the technology itself. However, faculty members must reach a minimum comfort level with the technology before they can realize the deeper educational benefits.

It is important to remember that technology is a tool to help, not the sole focus. Whether technology is a helping tool, an enabler, or a cost-effective tool, corporate trainers should emphasize the need to focus on teaching and learning and not on technology as an end in itself.

LANDMARK FOUR

Ensuring Success

There are no shortcuts; corporate trainers need to provide sufficient time for effectively implementing relevant training activities. Whereas Landmark 3 discussed some of the more technical aspects of designing and delivering corporate training, this landmark addresses success factors in implementation, such as building relationships across the organization, managing change, supporting training participants, and outlining expectations of employees.

Building Relationships Across the Organization

A key component to success in implementing an e-learning initiative is building relationships across the organization. Corporate trainers need to forge ties and work closely with other business

---

Directions for Your Journey

- Build strong relationships with other key business units in the organization.

- Adhere to traditional change management principles.

- Provide supportive learning environments for employees.

- Outline expectations for training participants.

---

units in the organization, especially IT, senior management, and HR. These ties are critical for any training effort to succeed. How corporate trainers would proceed depends on what audience they are serving; the following examples illustrate it.

For Booz Allen Hamilton, the critical roles in its learning strategies team draw on expertise throughout the organization. This collaboration demonstrates that the human infrastructure is as critical as the technology infrastructure at Booz Allen Hamilton. The essential roles are an instructional designer, a technology-training strategist, a trainer, and a project lead. In addition to working closely with individuals in these roles, corporate trainers have also forged a strong partnership with the IT staff. In many cases, the learning strategies team uses resources found in the other center teams. Performance consultants primarily perform needs assessments, but they share the results with the learning strategies team.

Procter & Gamble's e-learning team relies on support from other teams in the organization. An IT staff person resides on the e-learning team to provide support and perspective on technology implementations. Other key sponsors of the initiative from departments throughout the organization include:

- the chief information officer, who supported and provided funding for initial implementation;
- the vice president of global business solutions, who provided IT support for the team and capital to purchase the learning management system and live-distance licenses;
- senior HR executives, who allowed the e-learning team to pursue the vision; and
- vice presidents and general managers, who supported the development and deployment of a Web-based college.

Marketing and Communication

Corporate trainers need a comprehensive communications plan that targets the appropriate audiences and explains the most effective ways to take advantage of available training activities.

Communication efforts typically begin when creating a strategic approach for new or existing training. Many internal champions of various skills or content areas are not familiar with the costs and benefits of different instructional delivery options. It is important to employ dedicated personnel to address these concerns. By communicating the plans, objectives, and benefits of corporate training well in advance to the organization, employees will feel prepared and respond better to training activities.

Also, because different training activities require different skill sets, it is important to manage the people involved with developing content effectively. APQC advises building time and resources into working with training champions to get training developed on time and on budget.

Corporate trainers can benefit from inviting a representative from the marketing staff to be involved in gaining senior management support and then delivering training activities. This close relationship enables the marketing team to better understand the benefits of corporate training and develop messages for the appropriate audience. The marketing person or team should work closely with corporate trainers to survey the audience and segment it. Messages regarding the efforts can then be targeted to a particular group, which can increase their effectiveness in drawing the work force to the available training activities.

TRAVELER'S TIP

Potential Communication Tools

- Conferences
- E-mail
- Internet
- Intranet
- Live demonstrations
- Newsletter
- Road shows
- Staff meeting
- Surveys
- Videos
- Web sites

For example, working closely with its e-learning team, General Motor's marketing group developed a house and family brand for marketing learning strategies, including e-learning. They developed three basic strategies used in everything related to learning: communication, promotion, and operational strategies. Each strategy drives how they approach audience segments, be it GM management, stakeholders, or customers. The marketing strategy includes the organizational readiness activities, which marketing helps to execute. College development team members, in conjunction with the operations team, come up with the strategy in terms of organizational readiness, and marketing helps by developing the materials around that strategy. The focus of each strategy is reaching results and developing organizational capabilities.

The marketing and corporate university teams at General Motors staged the rollout of internal materials through the various internal communication channels and resource materials, such as a video. Initially, they focused on developing the business case for the leaders and management audiences.

Creating a Supportive Learning Environment

Marketing will be effective only if corporate trainers have worked with HR and senior management to ensure employees have a supportive learning environment. As evidenced in APQC's Best-practice Report *Technology-mediated Learning* (2000), many best-practice organizations provide support before, during, and after training activities. As a component of the overall training and support, corporate trainers may also want to consider providing library and information searches and management services.

Support before a training activity may involve showing participants how to apply tools used in the activity, testing proficiency on the subject to determine exactly what the participant needs to learn, and holding "boot camp" meetings for participants who need preparation before being up-to-speed with other participants in an upcoming training activity. The participant should be informed of what to expect, what equipment is required, and what the corporate trainer expects in return. (More on what is expected of students is provided in the following section.)

Support during participation in a training activity, be it ongoing or a one-time event, may include self-assessment tests, exercises, access to support tools, sample files, and opportunities to increase their skill level. For some learning opportunities, a chat room may be appropriate so that participants can discuss assignments and share experiences.

Support after participation in a training activity may include reference materials, a database of participants, a help desk or contact for additional questions, and continued communication as a way to maintain the sense of community developed among the participants and trainer.

To facilitate a learning environment, the Army Management Staff College provides nametags that identify participants as students. The college also encourages students to display their current work-load and project plans in a location where supervisors can readily view them. It suggests that students conduct their e-learning coursework in a separate cube at work to reduce distractions. The Army Management Staff College also recommends that students create a sign indicating that they are conducting course assignments while at work. At the beginning of a course, the Army Management Staff College informs participants' supervisors of the approximate length of time the course will consume.

Supervisor support varies for e-learning. Therefore, the Army Management Staff College conducts supervisor surveys to assess how many supervisors are graduates of the course themselves. Frequently, the supervisors who provide the most support to participants are graduates of the program (especially ones who were not supported by their own supervisor during the experience). Supportive supervisors understand how much value the course will add to the employee's development. Faculty members occasionally receive calls from supervisors who provide feedback on how effective the learning has been for their employees.

Outlining What Is Expected of Students

It is important for students to understand what is expected of them regarding their courses. Some training activities involve high levels of interaction, student participation, and information processing. Consequently, the participant must make cognitive and behavioral adjustments; these students need training on the use of any new technology, as well as on new forms of learning activities. Corporate trainers play a large role in establishing behavioral guidelines. Trainers should clearly set the expectations at the beginning of a training activity and reinforce these expectations and rules throughout the activity. Expectations may include:

- being an effective participant in discussion groups;
- giving and receiving feedback from other students;
- navigating through various forms of information;
- processing, interpreting, and synthesizing information; and
- collaborating for effective teamwork, when needed.

If expectations are not managed appropriately, then students may become disappointed or frustrated.

Evaluating Corporate Training Efforts

It is challenging to make a sensible evaluation of a corporate training effort. Schools have faced evaluation problems for years, and their solution—a testing method of evaluation—has not proven very effective. Because of an emphasis on testing, school instruction is often geared to the test that will be administered, and those subjects that are inherently testable are taught.

Be careful not to make the same mistake. Decide what it is important for employees to learn, but do not attempt to translate this into a set of learning objectives that define what an employee should know. Knowing and doing are not the same thing.

TRAVELER'S TIP

Determine how your organization will:
- measure the costs and benefits in the short and long term;
- measure quality, including effectiveness;
- measure service (availability and accessibility); and
- measure speed (responsiveness).

Organizations want employees who can behave properly, not ones who can recite the proper rules of behavior. The issue is not who completed the course or who had the best scores. The issue is who is now better at his or her job.

This landmark focuses on the evaluation methods organizations have put in place that may measure the performance of individuals, but have the primary purpose of gauging the overall corporate training effort.

Evaluation involves developing evaluation goals and timetables, using standardized data collection processes, defining roles and responsibility, and applying consistent approaches for analyzing and reporting data. With appropriate planning, a systematic and methodical approach ensures that measurement and evaluation receives proper emphasis throughout the design and development of a corporate training effort. These methods vary from the basic, smiley-sheet satisfaction evaluations to the more complex computations of a return on investment (ROI). The ultimate goal is to ensure that corporate training efforts are indeed supporting the organization's overarching strategies.

The Impetus for Evaluation

Why assess learning outcomes? Four reasons stand out: 1) to determine effectiveness, 2) to help improve instruction, 3) to be accountable to stakeholders, and 4) to help attract future customers or clients.

Assessing the end-of-course knowledge and skills a student or trainee possesses and establishing what part of the knowledge and skills were learned in the course or training program are two different tasks. Measuring learning gains requires pre-instruction measures to compare end-of-instruction results. Proving the gains takes time and money and presents technical challenges in legitimately ruling out causes other than the instruction.

The requirements of good assessment present a challenge to those who teach. In addition, employees in training vary enormously in characteristics that affect their potential for learning. A recent study on risk and promise among working adults found that at least 18 factors besides traditionally studied demographic differences have statistically significant effects on such measures of success as grades, ratio of courses completed to courses attempted, and semesters completed. Mapping issues that teaching and support personnel face in helping such diverse students succeed reveals the inadequacy of programs built on the idea that one size can fit all.

In addition to the diversity of student characteristics is the diversity of environments in which students and employees learn. The normal working adult has at least three primary environments impacting the likelihood of effective learning—work, home, and school. Determining what type of student works best in what type of environment is challenging for instructors, but important.

In addition, instructors must be able to sense what type of instruction their students respond best to. For example, they might note that some students in their class respond best to individual assignments, whereas others excel in a group environment.

To improve, an instructor must know what results he or she is getting, use clues to past successes and failures to devise improvements, and check their hunches for the next round of improvement efforts. Instructors' supervisors should make similar efforts and collaborate with the instructors to enhance results. The previously identified challenges provide a sense of the difficulty of this work, but the rising demands of global competitiveness for enterprises and job competition for individuals make clear the urgency of progress toward coping with these challenges.

One of the benefits of benchmarking the assessment of train-ing activities is the opportunity to learn how others have handled challenges and obstacles in the use of outcomes data for instruction improvement. For example, the study team discovered through site visits that decentralizing assessment places ownership of the findings and insight into their meaning in the hands of those most involved in instruction and curricula development. This increases the likelihood that practical ways to improve will be found and promptly applied.

In a nutshell, the four benefits of assessing learning outcomes are in knowing the product, using that knowledge to improve the product continuously, being able to give a good accounting of corporate training's labors and their costs, and attracting a continuing clientele. The four benefits are closely intertwined, and their enhancement is significantly aided by shared efforts to learn and adapt best practices.

Adapting Evaluation to the Culture of the Organization

Traditionally, objectives for corporate training efforts have focused on reaction and learning. More recently, objectives have been established for application and impact. Multiple objectives serve as a driving force behind the design, development, and delivery of any training program. It is useful to employ a variety of measurement techniques to evaluate an overall corporate training effort.

Formal methods for that evaluation vary but can include course evaluations, usage reports, pass/fail rates, completion rates, net present value, after-tax savings, and participant satisfaction surveys. Informal methods of evaluating the success of the effort include advisory councils, meetings to gather feedback and share best practices, numerous requests for new courses, focus groups, and observations. The measures will serve to drive changes in the program, determine the budget for corporate training activities, and to some extent, determine the ROI.

Best-practice organizations recognize that even though evaluation is a micro-level activity, there is a strong need to combine evaluation data to develop a macro-level view of the impact of the corporate training program.

Historically, evaluation has been approached from a micro-level analysis (one activity is evaluated). It is difficult to evaluate several activities at the same time or the success of all of the participants in a specific program over an extended time span. However, executives need more information than is often contained in a micro-level evaluation. They need some assurance that corporate training efforts are contributing overall.

TRAVELER'S TIP

Identify and report the impact of learning measurements by:

- incorporating a variety of methods to measure the impact of learning. Effective measurement programs incorporate: interviews, focus groups, questionnaires, action plans, contract performance, pre- and post-tests, on-the-job assessments, and performance results. (The most difficult aspect of training measurement is deciding which method to use and when to use it.)

- using a variety of performance improvement tools. Companies have hundreds of methods and tools to choose from.

- setting up evaluation programs to measure each learning activity. Every organization measures the impact of learning differently. Find out how successful organizations use a variety of methods to measure the impact on the employee, and see how they aggregate this information to understand the impact on the entire organization.

As the following examples demonstrate, organizations vary in the scope of their evaluation efforts. One thing is clear, however; regardless of where they are in of their evaluation efforts, these efforts are driven by what is important to the culture of the organization.

The Army Management Staff College varies its learning assessment methods according to the modules being assessed. Student, graduate, and supervisor surveys are conducted for all programs and tailored to the specific goals and objectives of each program. The college uses the following methods to evaluate the success of e-learning:

- a multifaceted evaluation process,
- student surveys completed at the end of each resident session and each of the four modules,

- graduate surveys conducted nine months after completion of the program,
- graduates' supervisor surveys completed one year after graduation, and
- e-campus user surveys (which can be submitted at any time).

The Army Management Staff College uses several other types of surveys to assess readiness, work environment, and supervisor graduation rates. Methods of assessment vary between the resident and nonresident programs. Resident students are assessed via six tests, two papers, and 16 feedback-only assignments such as papers and briefings. Nonresident students have 32 written requirements, such as essays, letters to editors, book analyses, and journal article summaries.

One of the course deliverables involves a writing requirement for students to address their own learning processes and outcomes. Army Management Staff College faculty members note positive behavioral changes between initial and concluding resident weeks. In addition, students report their use of newly learned skills and knowledge on the job as they readily apply what they have learned.

Following the conclusion of the course, the Army Management Staff College collects students' feedback about the program, curriculum, technology, and faculty. The surveys completed by nonresident students are almost identical to those used for resident students. Data from the master personnel database tracks graduates and provides the Army Management Staff College with quarterly updates of their progress. Since the college began posting all conducted surveys online, it has received more detailed comments and feedback. The surveys include both ratings (on the Likert scale) and comment boxes. Results are tracked in a database, and feedback is sent to the appropriate individuals to incorporate into future plans.

The Army Management Staff College conducts supervisor surveys to assess how many supervisors are graduates of the course. Additionally, faculty members occasionally receive anecdotal evidence in the form of calls from supervisors, who provide feedback on how effective the learning has been for their employees.

An initial survey assessment at the college provided information about how to focus future improvement efforts. Results of the survey indicated a desire for more interaction between students and faculty and revealed that if the faculty does not use and encourage the new technology, then students would not use it. Only students responded to the surveys, as faculty members tend to debrief face-to-face following the conclusion of courses.

In another example, one of IBM's four technology-enabled learning principles is that success will be substantiated through business measurements and impact. IBM achieved a cost savings of $350 million in 2000 because of its increase in distributed learning. It also saw a 2,284 percent ROI on its manager training e-learning initiative.

By focusing on measures that demonstrate added value or reduced cost, IBM uses the following measures to evaluate the success of e-learning:

- usage across 25 programs or curricula,
- usage compared to cost of student days and savings to IBM, and
- surveys that assess different aspects of several programs.

In terms of e-learning program measurement and evaluation, IBM uses the same four-level approach it uses for its management development program, which is similar to Kirkpatrick's four levels of evaluation (see the next section for a description of Kirkpatrick's framework).

In November and December of 2000, IBM's learning integrators interviewed more than 70 employees representing all business units and geographic boundaries for input. Results indicated that employees valued access to learning, a variety of learning approaches, the need to measure success through business results, and a desire to ensure accountability. Currently, learning integrators follow up with the participant's business manager at three- and six-month intervals following the conclusion of the course to assess progress. But it is not easy to tie learning to business results.

To measure leadership, IBM uses mastery tests and program surveys and assesses climate results from 360-degree feedback. To measure acceptance and use of e-learning, IBM tracks Web use and benchmarks with organizations such as ASTD and the MASIE Center. To measure ROI, IBM measures cost effectiveness, cost avoidance, and results enhancement. IBM has succeeded in lowering the cost of education per day by 17 percent.

These organizations have made progress measuring the application and impact of learning, but most are struggling to find a consistent, routine process. Finding the right mix of data collection methods and processes is a challenge for corporate trainers. In many cases, companies waste time and money because they do not plan a consistent process. Others waste time and money because they collect data they do not need or because the process they use to evaluate is unscientific and open to interpretation. To avoid such waste, it is important for organizations to standardize processes.

Fortunately, a variety of methodologies exist that help match a program's specific situation or environment to an appropriate evaluation process. The methodologies clarify issues such as accuracy, disruption of normal work activities, cost, and culture. Some of these methods include follow-up surveys and observation on the job. Other examples of methods that many organizations use to collect and assess data are listed in Figure 3.

Another important issue is finding a consistent process to isolate the effects of a program. There are many influences driving business impact measures; training activities are only one. A process should isolate the effects, even if it is only an estimation of how much of the improvement actually relates to the program.

It is a tremendous challenge for corporate trainers to find an accurate and reliable process that does not consume precious

Methods of Data Collection

Follow-up surveys/questionnaires
Observation on the job
Interviews with participants
Follow-up focus groups
Program assignments
Action planning
Performance contracting
Program follow-up sessions
Performance monitoring
Interviews with participant's manager
Preliminary and post-testing
Analysis of before and after individual performance measures

Figure 3

resources. The best strategy is to plan carefully, use shortcuts, and develop an internal culture around specific methodologies for collecting data and isolating the effects of the process.

A Framework for Measurement

Probably the most well-known framework for classifying areas of evaluation, Donald Kirkpatrick's framework contains four levels of evaluation. This conceptual framework assists in determining the types of data to collect and answers four important questions. (Another level, return on investment, has recently been added to the framework.)

1. **Reaction**—Were the participants pleased with the program?
2. **Learning**—What did the participants learn in the program?
3. **Behavior**—Did the participants change their behavior based on what was learned?

4. **Results**—Did the change in behavior positively affect the organization?
5. **Return on investments**—What was the monetary value of the results and costs for the program?

- **Level one:** Reaction involves how the participants judge the program's materials, instructors, facilities, methodology, content, etc. Participant reaction is sometimes a critical factor in redesigning or continuing human resources development (HRD) programs. The responses of a few very satisfied or disgruntled participants on reaction questionnaires can affect decisions.
- **Level two:** Learning evaluation involves measuring the extent to which principles, facts, techniques, and skills have been acquired. There are many different measures of learning, including paper-and-pencil tests, skill practices, and job simulations.
- **Level three:** Behavioral change is measured to determine the extent to which skills and knowledge learned in the program translate into improved performance on the job. Evaluations in this category include self-assessments and before-and-after comparisons of observations from the participant's superiors, subordinates, and peers.
- **Level four:** Evaluation of results involves monitoring organizational improvement through cost savings, work output changes, and quality changes.
- **Level five:** Return on investment (ROI) has recently become an additional level to Kirkpatrick's model. At level five, the framework compares monetary benefits from the program with its costs. Although the ROI can be expressed in several ways, it is usually presented as a percentage or as a cost/benefit ratio. (The next section addresses the challenges in determining an ROI.)

Ernst & Young, LLP Global Learning Solutions measures education and training outcomes with a system based on Donald

Kirkpatrick's four-level model of evaluation. This system measures the effectiveness of Global Learning Solutions learning solutions for various educational-delivery channels that incorporate technology (e.g., face-to-face, online, and CD-ROM).

Level one evaluations measure participant reaction by addressing how people feel about the learning solutions' relevance and the general experience. Global Learning Solutions measures all dimensions of the student's experience, including overall effectiveness, design of the program, the delivery vehicle, and anticipated impact. The data is reported through the intranet to various stakeholders (project managers, course developers, managers, and clients).

Global Learning Solutions measures the second level student improvement through reference tests. In courses where learning objectives focus on processes or products, performance tests measure students' acquired knowledge and skills. However, Global Learning Solutions typically measures student performance in the work environment, where the change can be evaluated in a larger context.

Level three measures performance on a case-by-case basis. Surveys are sent to students and their supervisors after the learning experience. The surveys contain rating scales and open-ended questions designed to measure application of the knowledge and

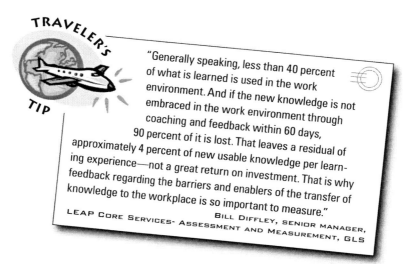

TRAVELER'S TIP

"Generally speaking, less than 40 percent of what is learned is used in the work environment. And if the new knowledge is not embraced in the work environment through coaching and feedback within 60 days, 90 percent of it is lost. That leaves a residual of approximately 4 percent of new usable knowledge per learning experience—not a great return on investment. That is why feedback regarding the barriers and enablers of the transfer of knowledge to the workplace is so important to measure."
— BILL DIFFLEY, SENIOR MANAGER, LEAP CORE SERVICES- ASSESSMENT AND MEASUREMENT, GLS

skills acquired in the course, increased confidence in performance, and impact on work performance. Particular attention is paid to the barriers and support for the transfer of course knowledge to the employee's work environment.

Global Learning Solutions uses an additional method of collecting level three assessment data. It selects a sample of the learning group and tracks the sample using participant-completed electronic logs. The logs document application and usage and are verified by a supervisor or manager.

Kirkpatrick's level four evaluation looks at the business impact of education. Global Learning Solutions examines business outcomes that may be linked to the individual, which in turn, may have resulted from training and education. Measures include retention, efficiency, and increased productivity. Global Learning Solutions also plans to monitor how learning links to variables such as program design, program delivery, and performance change.

Global Learning Solutions conducts a level one evaluation on every course taught; level two evaluations are performed on fewer courses. The percentage of courses that go through level three and four assessment is lower. However, Global Learning Solutions is aggressively implementing Kirkpatrick's measurement model for thousands of courses. Ernst & Young is dramatically increasing the percentage of level three and four measurement while balancing the need for measurement with cost considerations.

Return on Investment

Many organizations want to use ROI as a measurement tool but struggle to define how to calculate it and what to do with the results. Corporate training investments can be substantial, and measuring the payoff of that investment is a financially sound approach. Senior managers have ROI data to measure the payback of other types of investments, and they are demanding that corporate trainers use the same tool. Senior executives should receive results in terms they understand and appreciate, and an ROI calculation quantifies the value of training by comparing benefits with the cost of, or investment in, programs.

When comparing ROI calculations in best-practice organizations APQC has benchmarked, it was difficult to identify what inputs were used in the calculation and to ascertain exactly what the resulting ROI number meant. Furthermore, APQC found that in many cases, the thought of calculating ROI conjures many fears, some of which follow.

- ROI is too complex for most users.
- ROI is expensive and consumes too many critical resources.
- A negative ROI will be disastrous.
- ROI is a passing fad.
- The training and development staff will resist ROI.
- ROI is not a credible process; it is too subjective.
- ROI cannot measure soft skills programs—only production and sales.
- It is not possible to isolate the influence of other factors.
- Our senior team may require ROI for every program.
- Data collection systems are inadequate for ROI.

Most of these fears are based on misconceptions and misunderstandings of the ROI process and can be addressed practically. By planning ahead and dedicating appropriate resources, organizations can successfully calculate ROI for any program.

Implementing a successful ROI process does require sophisticated analysis. Organizations wishing to calculate ROI need to isolate the effects of a particular program on output measures, and the output data must be converted to monetary value.

Another important step is to fully allocate costs of a particular program. Because ROI compares the actual net benefits of a program with the program's costs, there must be some mechanism to easily and routinely capture the costs for a specific program or a small number of activities. The following list shows the typical factors in an ROI calculation:

- needs analysis,
- development costs,
- program materials,
- instructor/facilitator costs,
- facilities costs,
- travel/lodging/meals,
- participant salaries and benefits,
- administrative/overhead costs, and
- evaluation costs.

Reporting Results

There is a need for executives and other stakeholder to be able to review results quickly and understand how they connect to business needs. This need has forced corporate trainers to take a macro-level view and roll up data to present a comprehensive scorecard of different types of information. Figure 4 shows one such scorecard. Different types of information provide a macro-level view of the impact of a corporate university. This scorecard presents different types of data and shows the extent to which programs are linked to business needs and are influencing output measures. Unfortunately, establishing this link may be one of the most difficult issues for corporate trainers to address.

Mountains of data can be collected as a result of assessment activities. The key is for corporate trainers to identify which assessment activities produced meaningful data that could be used to enhance individual and organizational learning.

Preparing for the Expenses

Measuring results is useful only if the information is accurate, and accurate information costs money. Corporate trainers should expect to commit significant resources to the measurement and

Example of Scorecard Measures for a Corporate University

Indicators
Number of employees trained
Training hours per employee
Investment as a percentage of the payroll
Costs per participant

Reaction and Planned Action
Percentage of programs evaluated at this level
Ratings on seven items vs. target
Percentage with action plans

Learning
Percentage of programs evaluated at this level
Types of measurements
Selk assessment rating on three items vs. targets
Pre/Post differences

Application
Percentage of programs evaluated at this level
Ratings on three items vs. target
Percentage of action plans complete
Barriers (list of top ten)
Enablers
Management support profile

Business Impact
Percentage of program evaluated at this level
Link with measures (list of top ten)
Types of measurement techniques
Types of methods to isolate the effects of programs
Investment perception

ROI
Percentage of programs evaluated at this level
ROI summary for each study
Methods of converting data to monetary values

Figure 4

evaluation process. Included in these resources is a variety of skill sets and roles that will make up the measurement and evaluation team.

Four percent to 5 percent of the training budget should be the target for many organizations as they improve the scope, consistency, and usefulness of the measurement and evaluation process, with costs ranging from $600,000 to $1 million for large organizations. However, it is estimated that most corporate trainers allocate less than one percent of their budgets to measurement and evaluation. Thus, the challenge is to increase the budget fivefold to reach the appropriate level. The good news is that increased funding can be generated from the pay-off of the additional measurement and evaluation. Cost savings can usually be realized from the evaluation process as data is used to make adjustments in existing programs, prevent value-diminished programs, and eliminate ineffective or inappropriate programs. These savings can be diverted into the measurement and evaluation process, which allows some corporate trainers to increase expenditures without increasing the overall budget.

In addition to committing significant resources to measurement and evaluation programs, corporate trainers should focus considerable resources on building and developing their measurement and evaluation teams with regard to skill sets and roles. Evaluation specialists operate as consultants and use other staff members throughout the process to deliver a successful effort. Whereas all stakeholders are responsible for measurement and evaluation, there are few measurement and evaluation specialists who provide a range of highly specialized services. The typical skill sets measurement evaluation specialists need include:

- planning for the evaluation,
- collecting evaluation data,
- isolating the effects of training,
- converting data to monetary values,
- monitoring program costs,
- analyzing data including calculating the ROI,

- presenting evaluation data,
- implementing the process,
- providing internal consulting, and
- teaching others the process.

The actual experience level will vary, as will the perspective and orientation. With some larger groups, highly technical specialists may be needed, such as a Ph.D. in the specialized area of evaluation. Also, individuals are needed with practical work experience and knowledge of finance and accounting and the operations of the organization. This important mixture is unique for each organization.

Evolving Measures

Measurement and evaluation programs must accommodate an organization's changing needs. If corporate trainers truly measure how efforts support strategic goals, then those measures will need to change as the goals do. For most measurement and evaluation teams, what worked last year may not work this year. The following examples demonstrate how measurement and evaluation programs evolve as changes take place within organizations.

Due to the changing nature of the mission, the training evaluation program at National Security Agency has gone through many iterations. Training began as a centralized process in which 14 professionals conducted extensive quarterly curriculum reviews, quantitative and qualitative evaluations of courses in all areas, and validation of hundreds of courses. It then became a decentralized process that was subordinated to other departments. In 1999 it returned to a centralized process in which assessment, measurement, and evaluation were consolidated. National Security Agency has secured better responsiveness and understanding of the evaluation process by:

- providing easy access to level one questionnaires,
- making questionnaires shorter,
- delivering surveys to the correct people,

- involving students in the evaluation process from the beginning,
- providing feedback to participants after the evaluation is completed, and
- explaining the impact of the evaluation process.

Assessment of the evaluation process is an important component of the Tennessee Valley Authority's training program, and it directly impacts the program's success. When evidence points to the need for change, the Tennessee Valley Authority adapts accordingly. For example, it modified its evaluation process in direct response to feedback from executives. As in all organizations, decision-maker buy-in plays a key role in the success of the Tennessee Valley Authority's training programs. The Tennessee Valley Authority found that although executives said they wanted quantitative demonstrations of positive business results at the micro-level (course level), few top executives would dedicate the time to become familiar with methodologies, assumptions, or chain of logic employed in the organization's studies. Scrutinizing details convinced few executives. Rather, they were impressed by macro and qualitative information. Although the quantitative data was important to satisfy executives' curiosity, most were more impressed by articles in major magazines about the success of the Tennessee Valley Authority's training or a positive comment overheard in the lunch line. As a result, its corporate university modified its evaluation strategy to include a wider range of inputs, including anecdotes, philosophical treatments, social comparison information, and detail on level three and level four studies.

Selecting Measures

There is no universal route to ensure reliability and validity of assessment activities and instruments. Many organizations emphasize using multiple methods of assessment, with each providing a piece of the puzzle and together creating a more accurate picture of student achievement. Finding the most appropriate mix of tools and techniques becomes the challenge, as opposed to finding the one perfect solution. Of course, it is important to ensure that each assessment method used serves the intended purpose and strategy and accurately measures what it is intended to measure.

Tying assessment activities to their purposes may require creating some instruments and procedures in house or outsourcing the task to an expert source. Developing multiple measures that avoid bias, conflict of interest, or unreliability is time well spent, as the many tools can complement one another. In assessments of widely sought knowledge and skills, professionally developed examinations are often the most reliable and least costly options available, but they must be studied for their fit with the organization's intended priorities. These examinations might be supplemented by performance evaluations, surveys, portfolio analysis, and capstone courses to give a holistic view of a student's skills and abilities. In businesses, it might mean using standard exams along with on-the-job evaluations. Additionally, self-assessment can be an

TRAVELER'S TIP

Popular measures include:
- student days,
- tuition fees,
- courses delivered,
- programs conducted,
- reduction in turnover for those receiving training,
- increased productivity (pre-post behavior assessment),
- increased skill in managing savings,
- instructor payroll costs savings,
- increased sales due to training targeted on key selling programs,
- expectation vs. proficiency,
- expectation vs. performance,
- expectation vs. importance, and
- profits vs. performance.

important part of a well-rounded assessment program in both business and education.

Using the Results

The primary purpose of obtaining and reporting evaluation results is to improve the organization and, in particular, its employees' learning. Accordingly, the findings are best used in non-punitive ways. Corporate trainers should fight the urge to use assessment as part of the reward-and-punishment system. Major resistance can sprout up from those creating the assessment methods and tools as well as from those being assessed.

Best-practice organizations APQC has benchmarked strive to use the results of all assessment activities strictly to enhance performance. Throughout the assessment process results that can be viewed as negative inevitably will be unveiled, such as instructors' perceptions of students' failings or student satisfaction scores that reflect poorly on a particular instructor. This is exactly the information that best-practice organizations want to uncover; the challenge becomes how to use this as an opportunity for improvement.

Meeting with those who need to improve the learning initiative quickly as a consequence of the assessment results makes a strong statement about the importance and mission of the assessment activities. Showcasing assessment as a tool for collecting meaningful data and making real change fosters buy-in from all of the key stakeholders, builds trust with constituents, and encourages continued participation in assessment activities.

To further remove any negative connotations associated with using assessment data, best-practice organizations have made a conscious decision not to link these results with formal performance appraisals or faculty evaluations. The hub of the assessment activities—whether it be a director, an office, or a committee—strives to act as a performance consultant to ensure that those using the data find a way to make their actions purely developmental and not punitive.

Remaining Relevant

There is always room for improvement. For corporate trainers, improvement requires applying the evaluation results to remain relevant, finding easy to expand and evolve, and adhering to common critical success factors.

Using Evaluation Data to Remain Relevant

Landmark 5 detailed how to evaluate corporate training efforts. Successful corporate training programs use this evaluation data in a variety of ways. Corporate trainers should freely share assessment findings with everyone who has a legitimate need to use them or a legitimate interest in knowing about them. Prompt and comprehensive reporting of assessment data can complete the training activity for which the work has been done. It can also convey an appreciation to various stakeholders who contributed to the activity. While respecting legal and privacy issues, individuals on the front lines should be able to review and use assessment data to create their own strategies for improvement.

Successful organizations pursue the philosophy "if it is not going to be used, it is not collected." Evaluation data collected in huge volumes and stored in files that are never accessed is mostly a thing of the past. Even in large quantities, data is collected, analyzed, and used in a variety of innovative ways. It is important for corporate trainers to build a repository of data to gauge trends and patterns. Specific actions may be required, such as process improvement in designing and delivering learning opportunities.

Sharing the data in a format that is both timely and easily understood also increases awareness of the assessment process, removes any air of secrecy, and alleviates any fears that the data will be used for punitive measures. In addition, pushing the assessment data out into the organization spreads the responsibility for change and increases the likelihood of action.

In a best-practice organization example, participant feedback is gathered from all learning activities at Tennessee Valley Authority's corporate university and housed in a database. The database connects to an online monitoring system that allows Tennessee Valley Authority to respond almost instantaneously to participant feedback. Once the feedback is gathered, trainer and project team reports are generated from the data. The trainer reports are distributed to all corporate trainers active during the past month and include statistics and norms on the courses and trainer. The project team reports are sent to the team that owns the course. They include statistics and norms, as well as recommendations over time. The two reports provide direct and timely feedback to those who can make changes in the course.

Tennessee Valley Authority is careful to ensure that data is reported so it has meaning for other people. If a report from the staff does not make sense to Tennessee Valley Authority's corporate university general manager, then it is not allowed to be presented to higher-level decision makers. The reports have to be simple and in the language of the executives, while reporting on only key items.

Ways to Evolve and Expand

The best-practice organizations APQC has benchmarked did not complete and perfect their design and configuration of corporate training efforts prior to implementing them. Each organization had a vision and/or an approach: an initial starting model, or structure, that it realized would have to be modified later. The original models were not much different from more traditional models, but there was the expectation that the models would change and evolve through experience. Expect corporate training efforts to be evolutionary and incremental rather than revolutionary. And look for ways to improve, not only through evaluation results, but also by continually benchmarking internally and externally. That is, join interest groups to monitor development in the corporate training arena.

Examples of Ways to Evolve

- Better measure the effects of corporate training on meeting the organization's goals.
- Capture leadership tidbits.
- Create basic-level tutorials.
- Develop an annotated central resource repository or needs-based content library.
- Expand technical resources.
- Fine-tune infrastructure needs.
- Initiate online guest speaker discussions.
- Develop a needs-based content library.
- Pilot additional custom courses.
- Populate new curriculum areas.
- Provide additional distance-learning capabilities.

Several years ago, for instance, the Tennessee Valley Authority benchmarked itself against several professional, best-practice organizations to determine how other organizations measure and evaluate the impact of learning. During this study, the Tennessee Valley Authority found considerable variance with respect to certain training activities. It found that none of the organizations could provide conclusive ROI estimates on major components of an education system at sustainable levels of investment. It also found that many of these companies made investment decisions on education and training based on macro-level inputs and qualitative data. Consequently, the Tennessee Valley Authority took its lessons and developed a unique strategy that was appropriate for its own organization.

New technologies also create new opportunities to expand and evolve. Keep up-to-date with new technologies and methods of delivery training activities. Conferences and training programs can reveal how other companies are approaching common challenges. Organizations also keep up-to-date by consulting with various experts in the field. Theories are continually developing in corporate training, and many of these theories not only provide insightful and useful information but also give companies different perspectives and philosophies.

Critical Success Factors

APQC has found a number of common critical success factors at best-practice corporate training functions it has benchmarked.

- Forge strong partnerships with the IT and HR staff from beginning to end.
- Be prepared to revise plans and strategies.
- Gain senior management support from the very beginning.
- Expect for implementation to take longer than originally planned.
- Keep learning opportunities as simple as possible for employees.

- Educate the organization about learning opportunities from senior management to general employees to start the adoption process.
- Do not let the technology cloud the fact that learning drives business results.
- Always focus on the interactive element.
- Stay focused on the end goal and/or vision.
- Be willing to take risks, but be smart about them.
- Develop champions at all levels and in multiple areas of the organization.
- Think about e-learning from the employee's perspective, not just in terms of IT or budget.
- Communication is key.
- Remember that there is always room for improvement.
- Do not to expect significant change immediately. Change takes time before it is readily accepted and embraced.
- Improve remote access, where needed.
- Keep the competency list short, and refrain from asking managers to predict future training needs more than a couple years in advance.
- Excessively communicate to the target audience.
- Establish clear measures and track progress.
- Strengthen corporate training efforts based on key stakeholder feedback.

About the Authors

Marisa Brown

Marisa Brown is the manager of APQC's Collaborative Learning Group. Since she joined the Center in January 1996, Brown has been integrally involved with the all aspects of multiclient benchmarking studies. Brown has managed some of APQC's largest consortium benchmarking studies in education and learning, marketing, and new product development. Recently, Brown led the consortium study *Improving New Product Development Performance and Practices.*

Prior to joining APQC, Brown was a director of marketing at a lighting manufacturing company and was responsible for its implementation of a ISO9000 quality system. Brown earned her MBA from the University of Texas at Austin, where she was a Dean's Award recipient. She also earned her bachelor of business administration degree from the University of Texas at Austin, majoring in finance and honors business.

Paige Leavitt

An editor and writer, Paige Leavitt has helped to produce and publish a number of APQC publications, including the Profile series and Best-practice Reports. She is the author of *Solving Problems in Schools: A Guide for Educators* (2003) and co-author of: *Capturing Critical Knowledge From a Shifting Work Force* (2003), the *Content Management* Passport Guide (2003), the *Competitive Intelligence* Passport Guide (2004), *Disaggregating Data in Schools* (2004), and *The Executive's Role in Knowledge Management* (2004).

Before joining APQC, Leavitt edited language arts textbooks for Holt, Rinehart & Winston. She earned a bachelor of arts degree from the University of Texas at Austin.

Darcy Lemons

Darcy Lemons is a project manager with APQC's Customer Solutions Group. Lemons manages both custom project work and multiclient process benchmarking studies and participated in APQC's *Succession Management* (2001) consortium benchmarking study as part of the project team. She is co-author of *Capturing Critical Knowledge from a Shifting Work Force* (APQC 2003).

Lemons earned a bachelor's degree in psychology at Texas Tech University, graduating magna cum laude. She continued her education at Texas Tech for three more years, earning a master's degree in interdisciplinary studies (education psychology, family psychology, and psychology).

Wes Vestal

Wesley Vestal is a senior knowledge management consultant at APQC. Vestal has worked extensively in designing and implementing improvement strategies, solutions, training courses, and measurement systems. He is responsible for all KM products/services in APQC's custom work and KM benchmarking research agenda. Vestal also develops and markets leadership-focused benchmarking studies, including *Developing Leaders at All Levels* (2000), *Succession Management* (2001), and *Talent Management* (2004), Vestal's work in knowledge management has also looked closely at the integration points among leadership development, talent management, and knowledge management processes and roles.

Vestal holds a bachelor's degree in history and political science from Trinity University.

About APQC

An internationally recognized resource for process and performance improvement, APQC helps organizations adapt to rapidly changing environments, build new and better ways to work, and succeed in a competitive marketplace. With a focus on benchmarking, knowledge management, metrics, performance measurement, and quality improvement initiatives, APQC works with its member organizations to identify best practices, discover effective methods of improvement, broadly disseminate findings, and connect individuals with one another and with the knowledge, training, and tools they need to succeed. Founded in 1977, APQC is a member-based nonprofit serving organizations around the world in all sectors of business, education, and government.

Today, APQC works with organizations across all industries to find practical, cost-effective solutions to drive productivity and quality improvement. APQC offers a variety of products and services including:

- consortium, custom, and metric benchmarking studies;
- publications, including books, Best-practice Reports, and implementation guides;
- computer-based, on-site, and custom training;
- consulting and facilitation services; and
- networking opportunities.

PUBLICATIONS

APQC is the preeminent source for cutting-edge organizational research and improvement information. Designed to ease your way to positive results, APQC publications come in many forms and cover a wide range of subjects.

Passport to Success Series

This low-priced series of paperbacks can guide you on what can be a difficult journey through somewhat foreign territory. Each book in this series provides readers with mechanisms to gauge their current status, understand the components of a successful initiative in a specific topic area, and determine how to proceed within their own organization.

Knowledge Management: *A Guide for Your Journey to Best-practice Processes* (2000)

Call Center Operations: *A Guide for Your Journey to Best-practice Processes* (2000)

Stages of Implementation: *A Guide for Your Journey to Knowledge Management Best Practices* (2000)

Competitive Intelligence: *A Guide for Your Journey to Best-practice Processes* (2004)

Customer Value Management: *A Guide for Your Journey to Best-practice Processes* (2001)

Benchmarking: *A Guide for Your Journey to Best-practice Processes* (2002)

Communities of Practice: *A Guide for Your Journey to Knowledge Management Best Practices* (2002)

Content Management: *A Guide for Your Journey to Knowledge Management Best Practices* (2003)

Succession Management: *A Guide for Your Journey to Best-practice Processes* (2004)

Corporate Training: *A Guide for Your Journey to Best-practice Processes* (2004)

New Product Development: *A Guide for Your Journey to Best-practice Processes* (2004)

Other popular books include *Building a Breakthrough Business* (2004), *Capturing Critical Knowledge from a Shifting Work Force* (2003), *Offshore Ready* (2004), and *The Executive's Role in Knowledge Management* (2004).

CD-ROM Training Series

APQC's Connected Learning™ series brings leading-edge processes, tools, and techniques to you and your organization through integrated delivery of curriculum customized to your needs. This series provides both the knowledge and skills employees need to excel, while offering the flexibility to get the training they need when they need it. Along with a number of new titles added in 2004, all of the courses have been updated with improved navigation features.

APQC's Connected Learning series offers comprehensive, integrated, CD-ROM training opportunities in knowledge management and the performance excellence. Titles include:

- *Benchmarking Overview,*
- *Benchmarking Skills,*
- *Building and Sustaining Communities of Practice,*
- *Complete Benchmarking Package,*
- *Content and Knowledge Management Systems,*
- *Developing a Measurement Framework,*
- *Establishing Performance Measures,*
- *Facilitating Change: Creating a Knowledge-Sharing Environment,*
- *Knowledge Management: Approaches to Implementation,*
- *Knowledge Management 101: An Overview,*
- *Knowledge Management Starter Kit,*
- *Knowledge Management Strategies and Tactics for Business Results,*
- *Knowledge Mapping,*
- *Measuring Your Knowledge Management Initiatives,*
- *Performance Excellence Starter Kit,* and
- *Process Mapping.*

Industry-specific Collections

Using its award-winning benchmarking methodology, APQC aggressively and comprehensively researches practices critical to the corporate world. Through these efforts, APQC has formed an impressive catalog of case studies from the world's leading organizations. APQC offers these case studies, organized by industry, on its *Continuous Improvement* series of CD-ROMs. Individuals interested in their industry's continuous improvement efforts will find this collection useful in gauging industry-wide trends and examining best practices in a spectrum of continuous improvement arenas, from knowledge management and performance measures to competitive intelligence and online training. Collections are available for:

- aerospace and airlines,
- chemicals,
- energy,
- financial services, and
- food and beverage,
- government agencies,
- health care,
- insurance,
- pharmaceuticals and biotechnology,
- technology, and
- telecommunications.

Best-practice Reports

This series of in-depth reports based on benchmarking studies consists of a detailed examination of study findings and case studies of leading organizations. Covering a wide range of topics in operational improvement, recent titles follow.

Building and Sustaining Communities of Practice
Business-to-Business Branding: Building the Brand Powerhouse
Deploying Six Sigma to Bolster Business Processes and the Bottom Line
Developing Competitively Superior Customer Relationships
Facilitated Transfer of Best Practices
Improving Growth and Profits through Relationship Marketing
Improving New Product Development Performance and Practices
Managing Content and Knowledge
Managing Marketing Assets for Sustained Returns
Maximizing Marketing ROI

Measuring the Impact of Knowledge Management
New Product Development: Gaining and Using Market Insight
Performance Measurement: Implementing the Balanced Scorecard
Planning, Implementing, and Evaluating E-Learning Initiatives
Project Management
Replicating Gains from Six Sigma and Lean
Retaining Valuable Knowledge: Proactive Strategies to Deal with a
Shifting Work Force
Succession Management: Identifying and Cultivating Tomorrow's Leaders
The Customer-centric Contact Center: A New Model
User-driven Competitive Intelligence: Crafting the Value Proposition
Using Knowledge Management to Drive Innovation
Using Science and Technology Intelligence to Drive Business Results
Virtual Collaboration: Enabling Teams and Communities of Practice
With many more to come in 2005

The Profile Series

APQC has introduced a new series of reports that captures information on a specific organization over the course of several benchmarking studies. Unlike a report that simply indicates an organization's current perspective, this series details research from the early days of improvement efforts through to the organization's mature outlook as it experiences success. Readers have an opportunity to examine how an organization began its improvement efforts, how its focus evolved, and what challenges it faced. This is an excellent way to compare your own organization's improvement efforts.

Titles in this series include: *The World Bank Profile: Best Practices in Knowledge Management*, *The Dow Profile: Process-focused Best Practices*, and *The Xerox Profile: Best Practices in Organizational Improvement*.

Learn more about the hundreds of publications available from APQC at www.apqc.org/pubs.